COPA SAVANNA! Is There Such A Word?

Earth Science Book Grade 3

Children's Earth Sciences Books

In this book, we're going to talk about savannas around the world. So, let's get right to it!

There's a famous beach in Brazil called the "copacabana." What about a "copa savanna"? Is there such a word? There isn't, but if there was, maybe it could be used to describe the huge expanse of savanna in Brazil.

View of Cerrado Biome

WHAT IS A BIOME?

A biome is a community of plants and animals living in a large habitat. Biomes are usually defined by their climate, soil, or geology. Within a biome, plants and animals have specific adaptations that have made it possible for them to survive and thrive.

Each biome has several different types of ecosystems. The major types of biomes are:

• Desert
• Aquatic
• Forest
• Grassland
• Tundra

Desert Biome

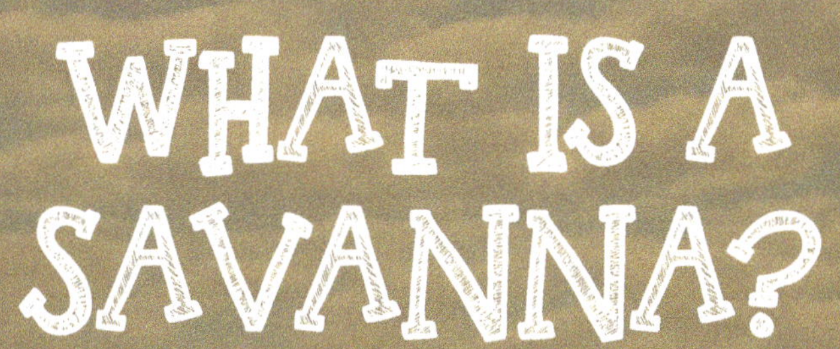

WHAT IS A SAVANNA?

Grassland biomes come in two main types: the savanna and the temperate. The savanna is often described as the tropical grasslands.

WHERE IN THE WORLD ARE SAVANNAS?

Savannas are generally situated close to the equator and this is one reason they are called "tropical." They are also mostly found in between the desert and the rainforest. Earth's largest savanna is found on the continent of Africa.

AFRICA

Savanna in Australia

The African savanna is so large that it covers almost 50% of the continent. South America has two areas of savannas as well. India and the northern region of Australia have savannas too. There are no savannas in the United States.

CHARACTERISTICS OF SAVANNAS

If you looked out on the wide expanse of the savanna, you would see different types of grasses, a shrub here and there, and a few scattered trees. Depending on the season, the weather will be quite different. During the rainy season, which is during the summertime, there are usually at least 15 inches and as many as 25 inches of rain.

During the dry season, which is during the wintertime, only a few inches of rain will fall. The summertime is warm and humid and the wintertime is much dryer and a little cooler.

Herds of animals that live on the different grasses of the savanna can be seen grazing. They have adapted to the climate and the vegetation that lives there.

Herd of Antelopes eating grass

Zebras

ANIMALS OF THE AFRICAN SAVANNA

The enormous herds of animals that graze on the grasses and trees of the African savanna are one of the Earth's most amazing sights. These plant-eaters, called herbivores, live here year round. Some of the herbivores that live in herds on the grasslands are:

- Zebras, which are African wild horses
- Wildebeests, which are a type of African antelope

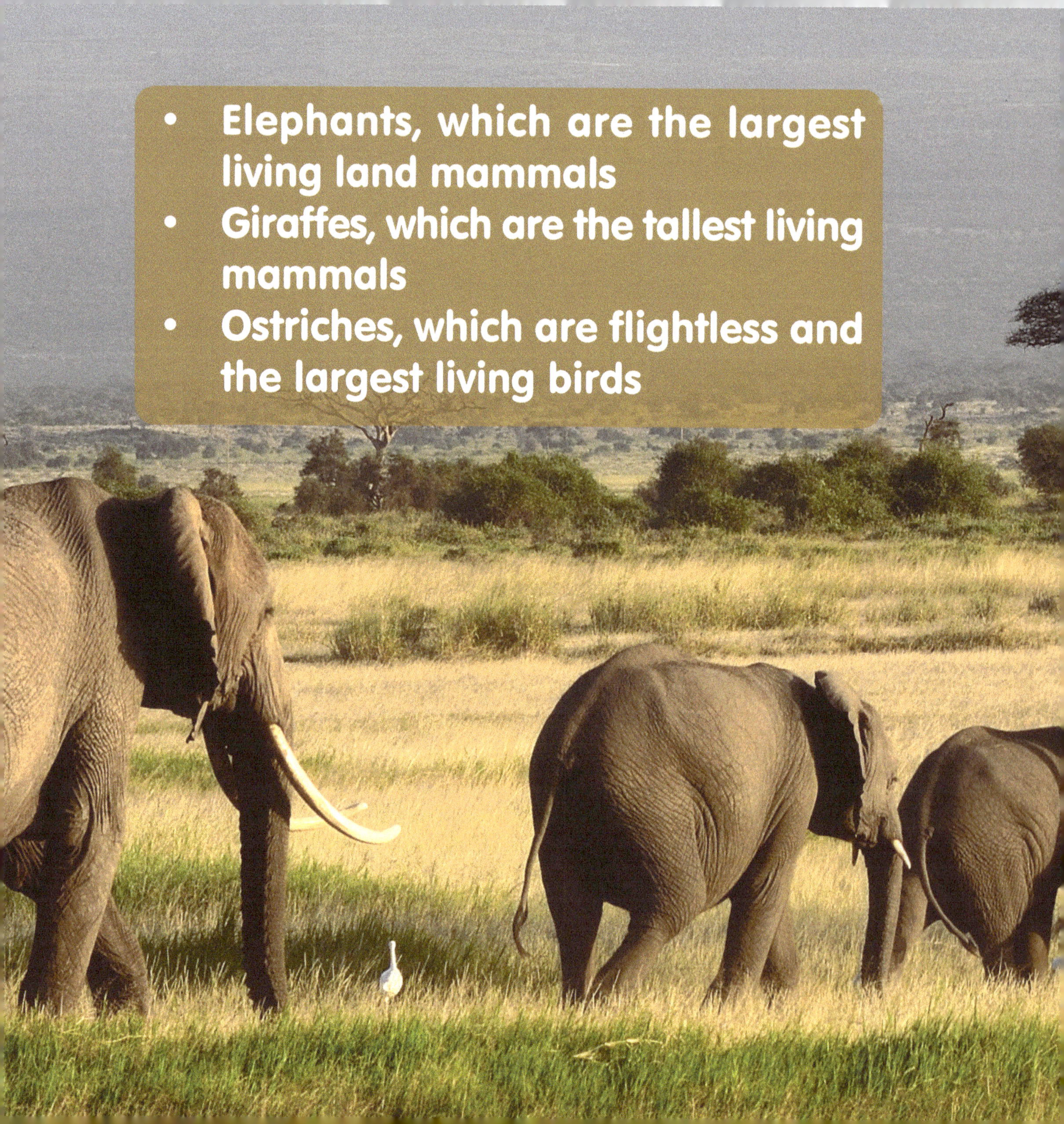

- Elephants, which are the largest living land mammals
- Giraffes, which are the tallest living mammals
- Ostriches, which are flightless and the largest living birds

Elephants

Cape Buffalo

- **Gazelles, which are a type of antelope found in both Africa and Asia**
- **Cape buffaloes, which are a type of cattle with enormous horns**

    One reason that the savanna can provide food for all these different herds is that there are many different types of grasses. Some animals, such as wildebeests, have adapted to eat the shorter grasses, while other animals, such as giraffes, have adapted to eat tree leaves.

Wildebeests

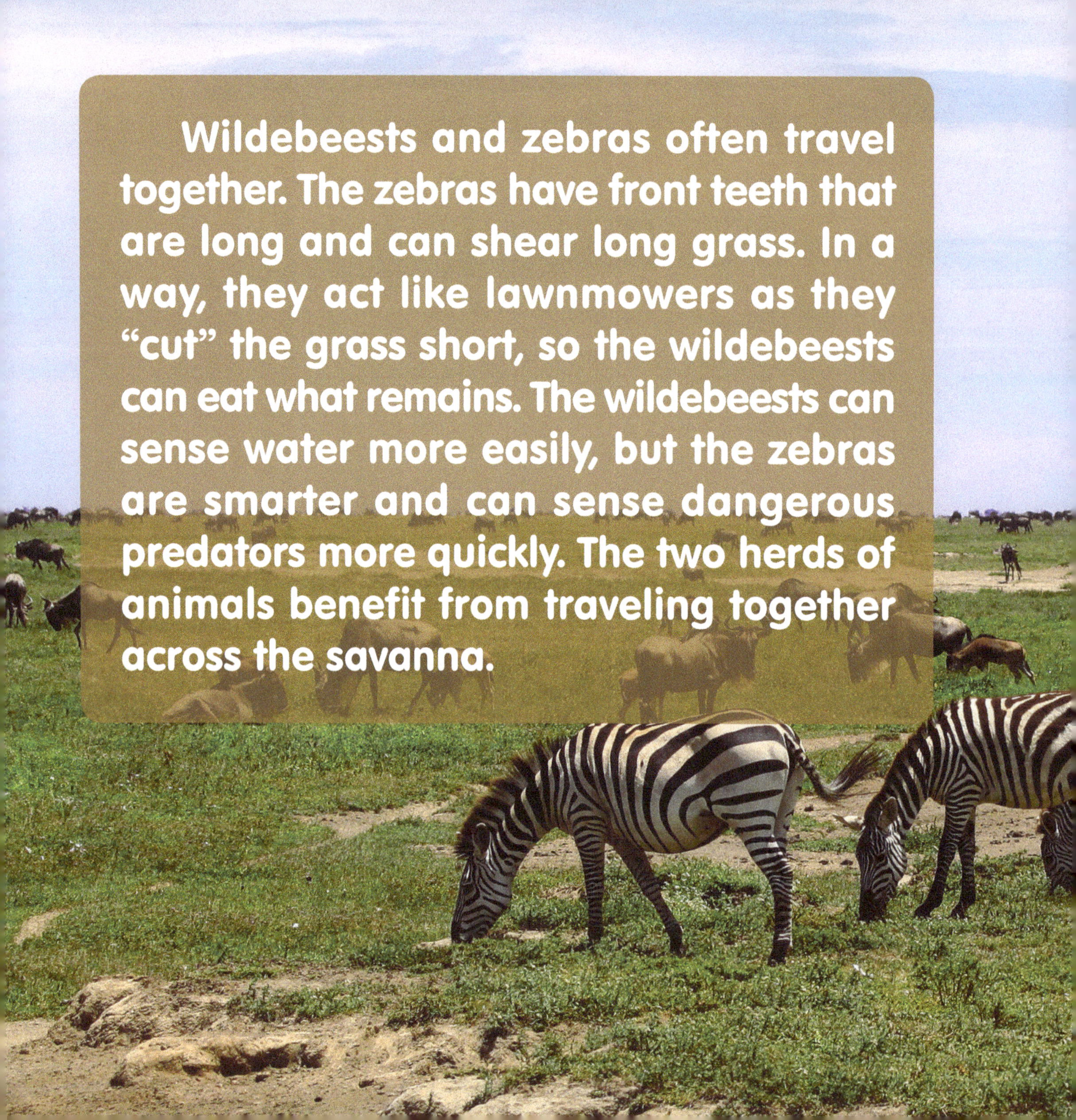
Wildebeests and zebras often travel together. The zebras have front teeth that are long and can shear long grass. In a way, they act like lawnmowers as they "cut" the grass short, so the wildebeests can eat what remains. The wildebeests can sense water more easily, but the zebras are smarter and can sense dangerous predators more quickly. The two herds of animals benefit from traveling together across the savanna.

Wildebeests and Zebras eating grass

Everything would be like paradise on the savanna for the large herds of herbivores if it weren't for the scary meat-eating predators. The plant-eating animals do their best to avoid predators. Giraffes are so tall that they can spot predators for miles away. Elephants are so big that when they stand together in their herds, few predators will dare to attack them. Gazelles and ostriches use their running skills to escape when predators are chasing them.

Gazelles and Ostrich

Cheetahs

The predators are all carnivorous, which means they eat meat instead of plants. The big cats—cheetahs, lions, and leopards—all have different hunting strategies. For example, the cheetah is the fastest animal on land. It can run at a top speed of 70 miles an hour for short periods of time to bring down a gazelle.

Other predators, such as lions, hunt in groups and try to get weaker herbivores separated from the herds so they will be alone and unprotected. Still others, like hyenas and vultures, eat the leftovers from the kills other predators have made. The deadly black mamba snake waits in the grass to strike at its victim. It hunts small mammals and rodents.

Lion

Baobab Tree

VEGETATION OF THE AFRICAN SAVANNA

Most of the vegetation on the savanna is grass. There are many different types including lemon, Rhodes, star, and Bermuda. The scattered trees include the acacia, the baobab, and the jackalberry. Just like the animals of the savanna, the savanna plants have adapted to survive in this environment. Some can store water as well as energy in their trunks, bulbs, or roots. Others have large root systems that go deep into the ground to tap sources of water under the soil.

WHY ARE FIRES IMPORTANT TO THE SAVANNA?

Fires are a critical part of savanna life. During dry spells, naturally started fires remove old grass and create the opportunity for new plants to grow. Many of the grasses will survive the fire, because they have adapted to have extensive root systems. The grasses will grow back quickly once the fire is out. The savanna trees have very thick bark that helps them survive during fires. Most savanna animals can outrun the fire. Smaller animals may dig burrows deep in the ground and stay there until the fire has passed over. Large numbers of insects die during fires, but their bodies are eaten by birds, rodents, and bats.

Cerrado Landscape

THE BRAZILIAN SAVANNA

The savanna area of Brazil is called the Cerrado, which is located in the central high plains area of Brazil. Although it's not as large as the African savanna, it's about three times the size of Texas. This huge biome is about one-fifth of the area of the country covering 1.2 million square miles of land.

Canyon Xingo of Sao Francisco River

The Cerrado is in danger of being destroyed due to farming and cattle ranching. It's a very important biome, but unfortunately it's one of the least protected regions in the country. The Cerrado provides water to three of the most important water basins in South America-- the Amazon basin, the Paraguay basin, and the Sao Francisco river basin.

It's also a region filled with an amazing diversity of plants and animals. It's believed to be the most biologically rich of all the world's savannas. Scientists estimate that there are over 10,000 different species of plants and about 50% of those species are not found anywhere else in the world. There are also about 400 different tree species and shrub species that are not found elsewhere.

Flowers from Cerrado

Giant Anteater

There are more than 900 different species of birds that make the Cerrado their home. The area also has many large mammals, almost 300 different species including some species that are currently endangered, such as the jaguar, the Cerrado fox, the giant anteater, the maned wolf, the marsh deer, and the pampas deer.

- Because there are extensive periods of wet and dry in the savanna, the food availability changes throughout the year. As a result, some animals migrate out of the savanna during the dry season.
- Many of the herbivores of the African savanna have long legs, which help them as they travel in their yearly migratory paths.

Sahara Desert

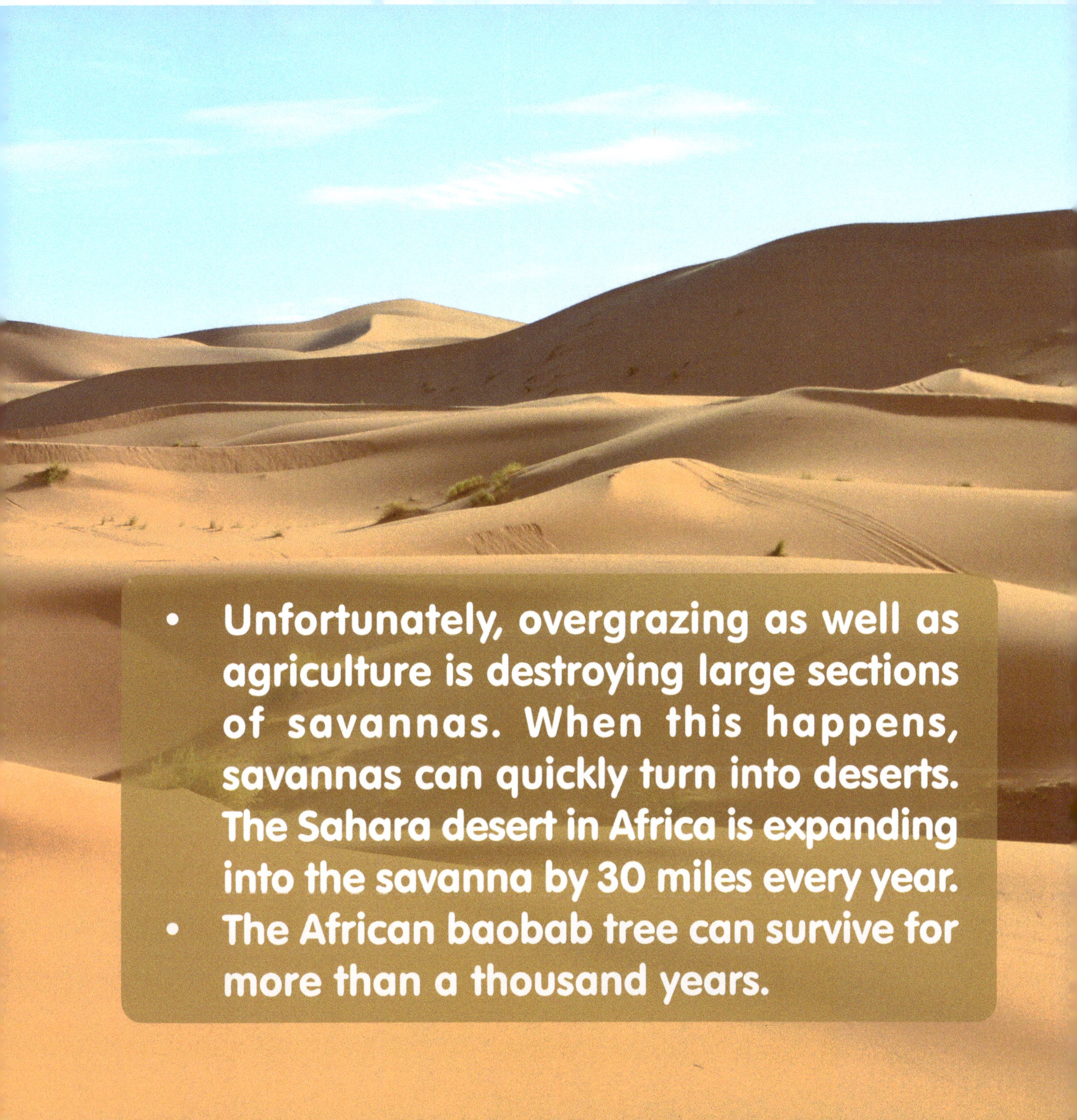

- Unfortunately, overgrazing as well as agriculture is destroying large sections of savannas. When this happens, savannas can quickly turn into deserts. The Sahara desert in Africa is expanding into the savanna by 30 miles every year.
- The African baobab tree can survive for more than a thousand years.

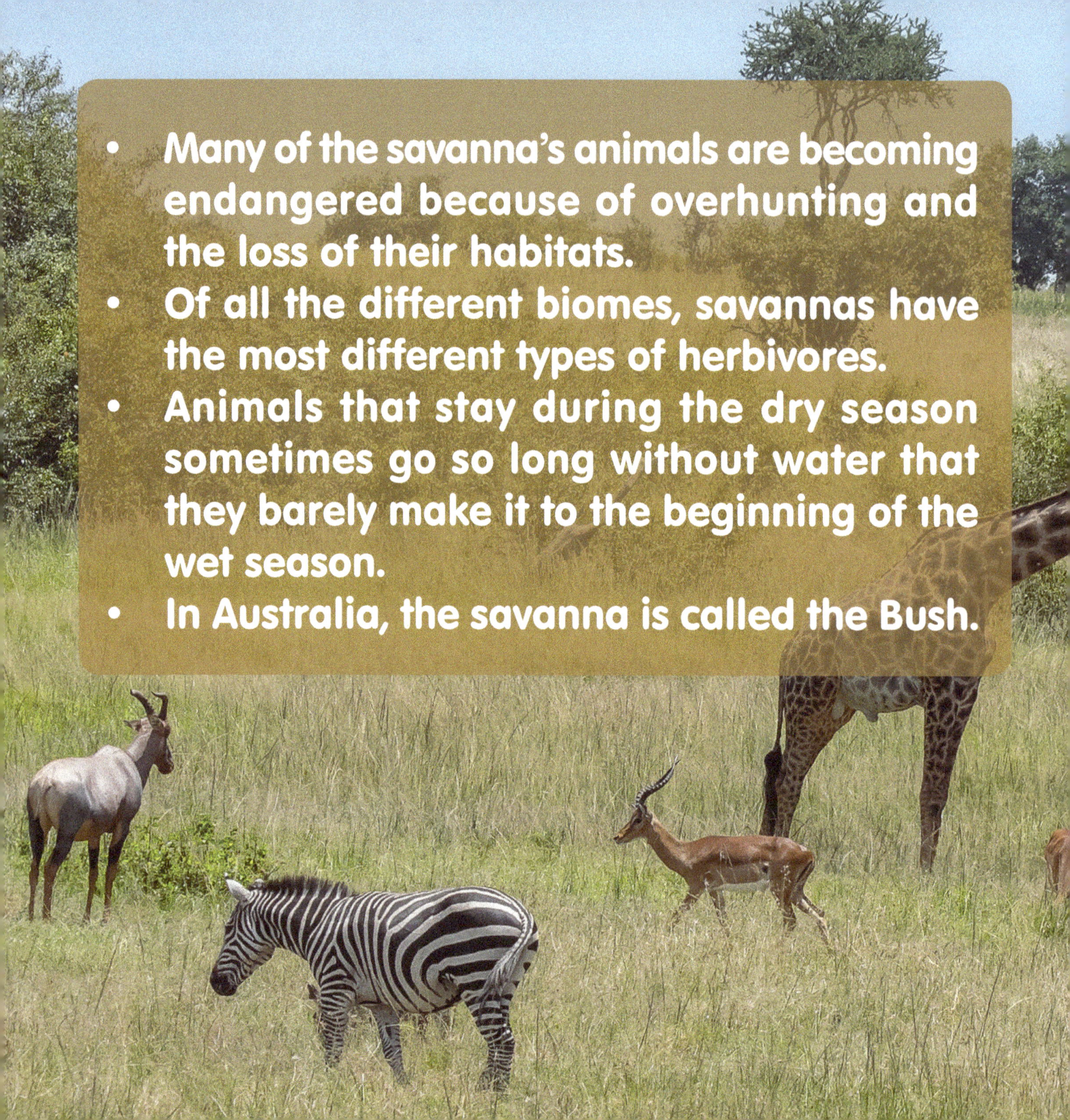

- Many of the savanna's animals are becoming endangered because of overhunting and the loss of their habitats.
- Of all the different biomes, savannas have the most different types of herbivores.
- Animals that stay during the dry season sometimes go so long without water that they barely make it to the beginning of the wet season.
- In Australia, the savanna is called the Bush.

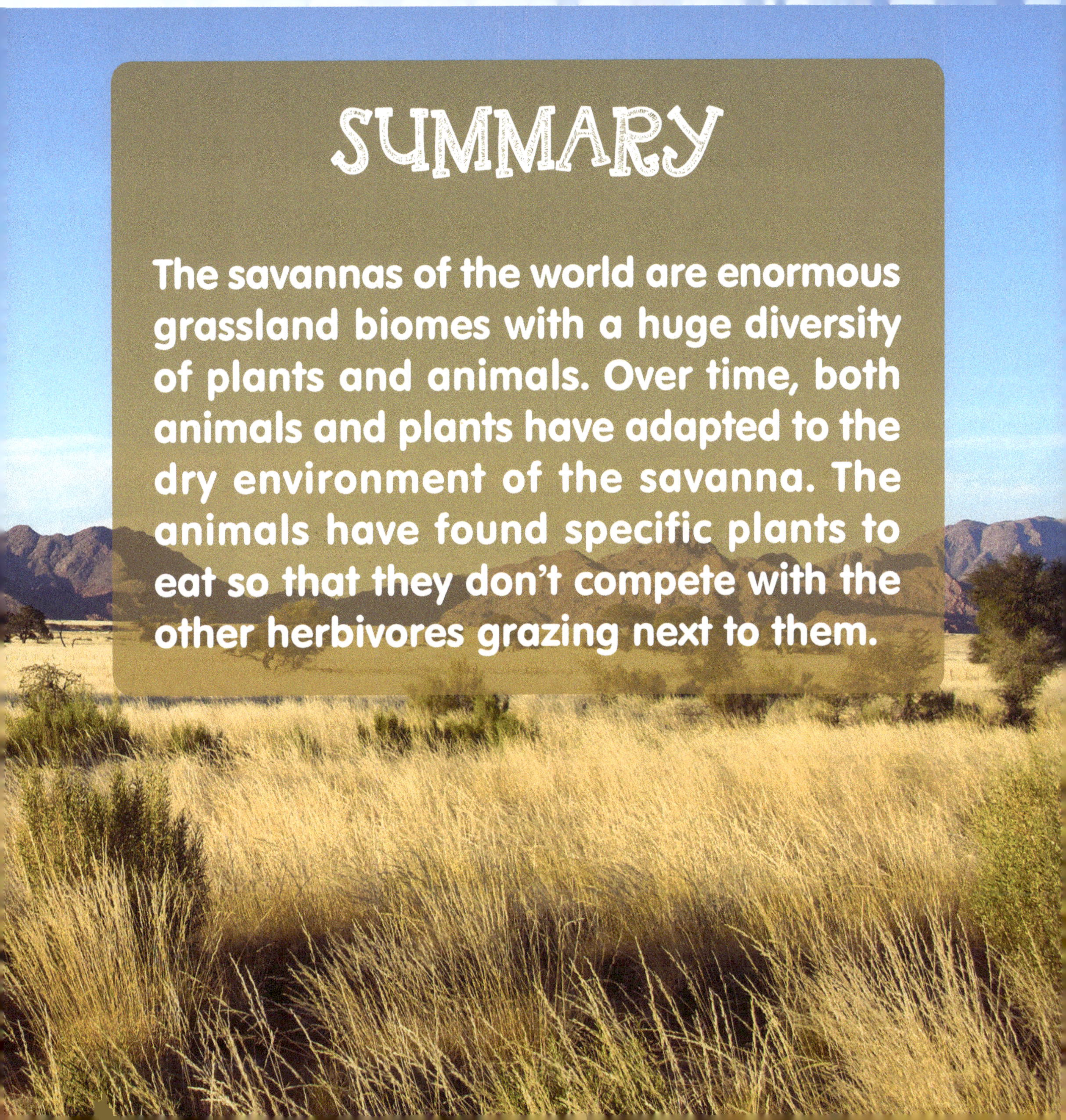

SUMMARY

The savannas of the world are enormous grassland biomes with a huge diversity of plants and animals. Over time, both animals and plants have adapted to the dry environment of the savanna. The animals have found specific plants to eat so that they don't compete with the other herbivores grazing next to them.

Their adaptations have allowed them to thrive even when living closely with many other herds of animals. Both herbivores and carnivores have adapted different strategies for survival.

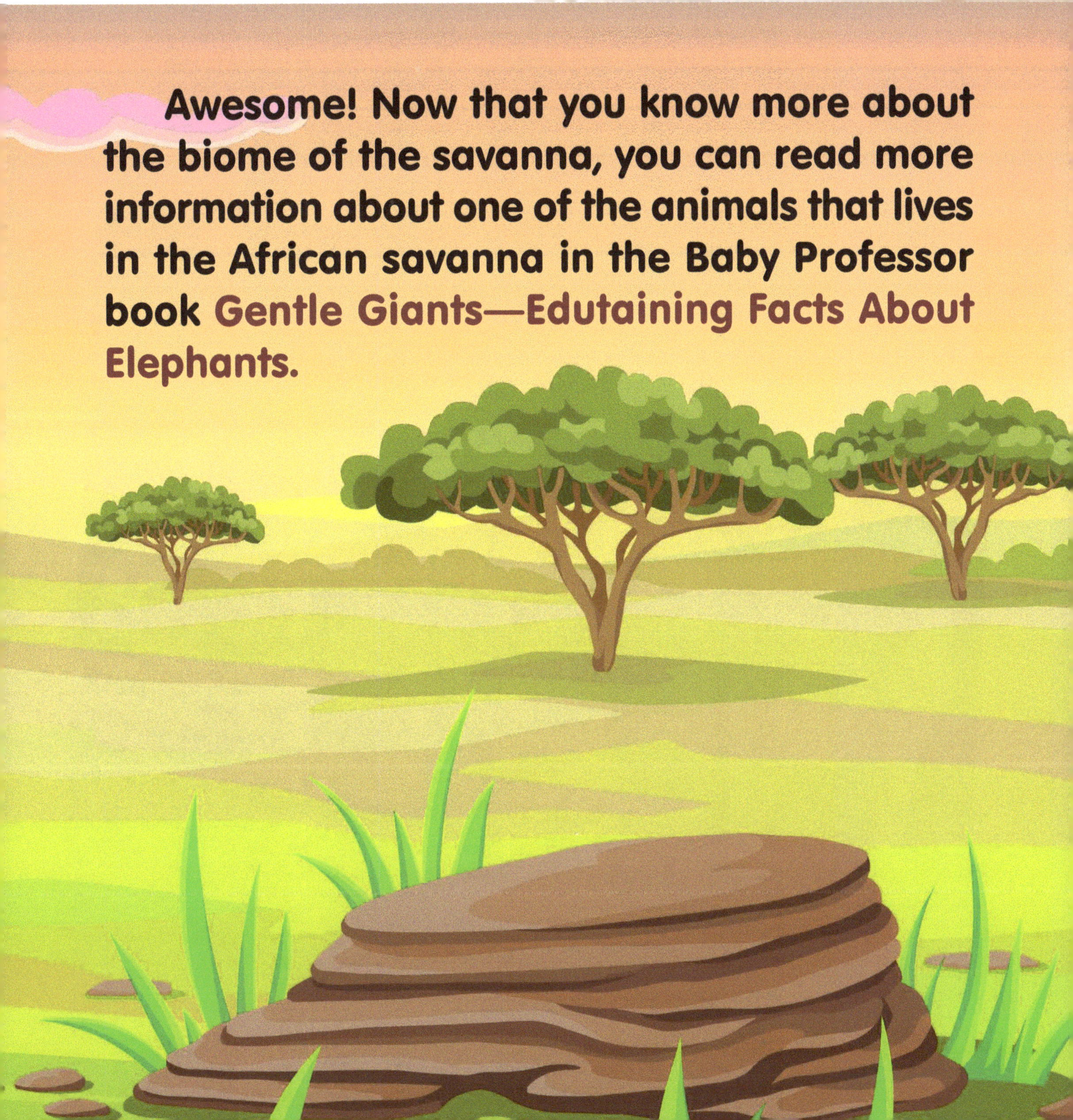

Awesome! Now that you know more about the biome of the savanna, you can read more information about one of the animals that lives in the African savanna in the Baby Professor book Gentle Giants—Edutaining Facts About Elephants.

Visit
BABY PROFESSOR
EDUCATION KIDS
www.BabyProfessorBooks.com
to download Free Baby Professor eBooks
and view our catalog of new and exciting
Children's Books